PRIVATE TOWERS

Title page: Valley View Silo, RoTo Architects
Photograph by Larry Stanley

First published in 2002 by HBI, an imprint of
HarperCollins Publishers
10 East 53rd Street
New York, New York 10022-5299

Distributed in the U.S. and Canada by
Watson-Guptill Publications
770 Broadway
New York, New York 10003-9595
Tel: (800) 451-1741
     (732) 363-4511 in NJ, AK, HI
Fax: (732) 363-0338

ISBN: 0-8230-4311-8

Distributed throughout the rest of the world by
HarperCollins International
10 East 53rd Street
New York, New York 10022-5299
Fax: (212) 207-7654

ISBN: 0-06-008761-7

Packaged by:
Grayson Publishing
1250 28th Street NW
Washington, DC 20007
Tel: (202) 337-1380
Fax: (202) 337-1381

Printed in Hong Kong
First Printing, 2002

1 2 3 4 5 6 7 8 9 /04 03 02

PRIVATE TOWERS

BY JAMES GRAYSON TRULOVE

CONTENTS

Mention towers and images come to mind of thick-walled turrets providing security for medieval castles, of skyscrapers, of bell towers, and of ranger stations in the midst of dense forests. From the top of a tower, one is master of the universe—or at least that part of the universe visible from the tower's vantage point. Piercing the sky, the tower can be a place of solitude and security, for reading, writing, and thinking. It also can be a familiar and welcoming marker in the landscape.

This book examines towers as a domestic phenomenon, whether as stand alone structures or incorporated into existing homes. Some of the projects presented in *Private Towers* are the realization of childhood dreams of living in a tree house or of living above the clouds. Others are practical, real-world solutions to complex architectural problems. Projects range from complete, self-contained homes such as the TowerHouse, the Pencil Tower, and the Valley View Silo to towers for viewing and contemplation like the Georgia Bar and the Bell Tower. The YardBird and the Loken Tower were designed to fulfill decidedly utilitarian functions of becoming home offices while The Cistern and the Rural Studio Silo are both remarkable examples of adaptive reuse of existing structures.

In all cases, the projects chosen for *Private Towers* are strikingly original in their design and execution. They illustrate how towers can often provide a practical and thoroughly satisfying solution to a unique building site or for a client with lofty requirements.

Left, Georgia Bar, AndersonMasonDale Architects
Photographer: Greg Hursley

PENCIL TOWER

Even in a city where space is at an extraordinary premium, the approximately 12-by-36-foot footprint for this five story Tokyo tower provided an uncommon challenge for the architect. The Pencil Tower has commercial space on the first and second floors with living accommodations above for a family of four. Climbing past the commercial space, one enters the residence on the third floor where the living and kitchen areas are located. The children's room is on the fourth floor and the master bedroom on the fifth. All rooms are open onto the stairwell. Elevated above the master bedroom is a small roof garden.

Viewed from the street, the commercial portion of the tower is concealed behind a floating concrete slab, with the spiral staircase to the residential quarters revealed at the bottom of this slab. The entrance to the business is on the ground floor to the right of the stairs. Above the slab, beginning at the third floor, the residence is sheathed in translucent glass with horizontal overlays.

Inside, the spiral stair cuts a wide vertical swath up through the building terminating at the roof garden. The strong emphasis on the vertical nature of the interior space reduces the usable floor area. And yet this bold vertical gesture, along with extensive use of glazing both on the walls and ceiling, creates the illusion of a far more spacious dwelling.

The interior is a monochrome of white punctuated by minimalist blond wood furniture designed by the architect. The stairs are thin slabs of steel and the floors are a soft, pale maple.

Akira Yoneda Architect
Photographer: Koji Okumura

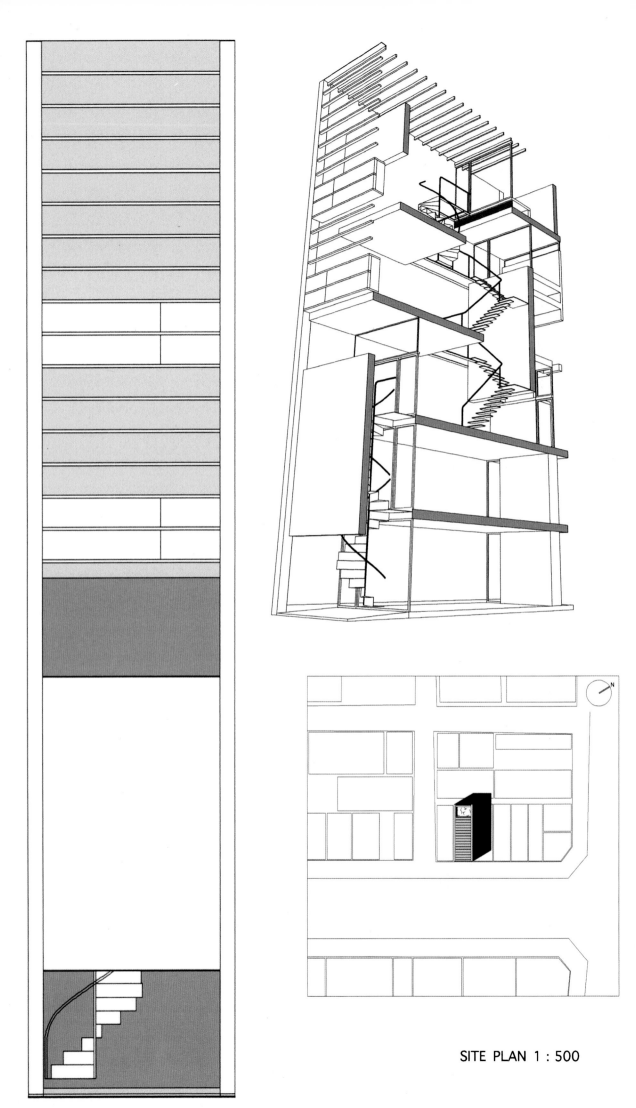

12 Pencil Tower

SITE PLAN 1 : 500

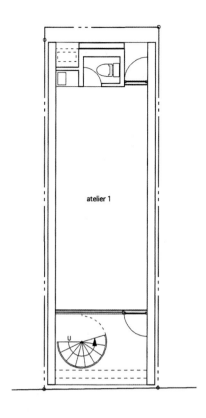

atelier 1

1F

atelier 2

2F

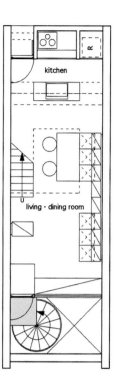

kitchen

living · dining room

3F

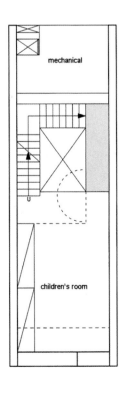

mechanical

children's room

4F

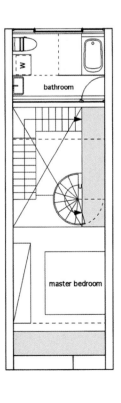

bathroom

master bedroom

5F

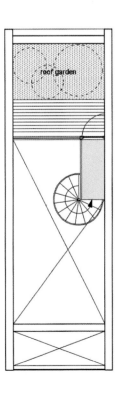

roof garden

RF

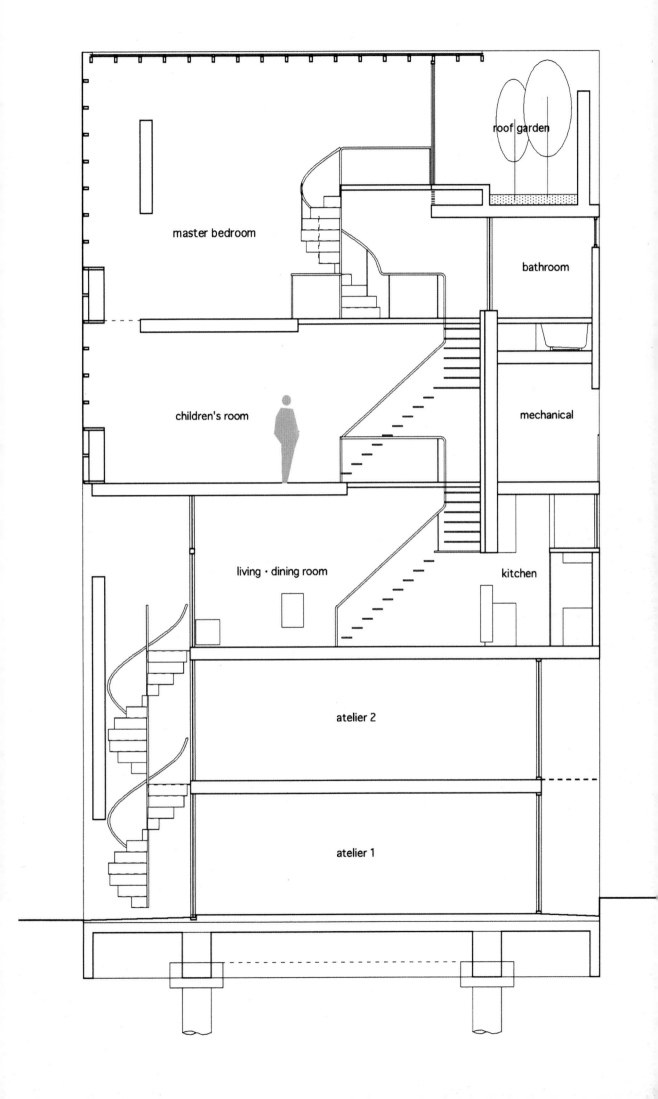

roof garden

master bedroom

bathroom

children's room

mechanical

living · dining room

kitchen

atelier 2

atelier 1

Above, a view up the stairwell to the glass roof. Right, a view down, to the living/kitchen area.

Previous pages, the master bedroom and children's bedroom. Left and above, the living/dining area viewed from the kitchen.

Above, the roof garden seen from the master bedroom. Right, the house glows like a Japanese lantern at night.

LOKEN TOWER

The idea for a tower addition to the existing house was the result of the owner's need for an home office in close proximity to the second-floor master bedroom. All adjacent bedrooms were spoken for so an addition was necessary. Because of the configuration of the first floor rooms and exterior decks, an attached two-story addition would have been disruptive. By designing a free-standing tower connected to the second floor via an enclosed bridge, the architect was able to leave the first-floor undisturbed. And as a bonus, the architect was free to orient the tower in such a way as to take advantage of remarkable views of Lake Superior to the southwest from the upper level. The structure's resemblance to a clock tower was not accidental: the owner is an avid antique clock collector.

The tower is sited on a steep hillside south of the house. The poured concrete foundation creates a fort-like space that becomes a play area for the children. The space under the connecting bridge provides a welcomed shaded area during the hot summer months. Inside, the bridge contains storage. On the first floor of the tower is a library accessible to the office through a floor hatch via a ships ladder fashioned after the cab access ladders used in the big mining trucks in the region.

David Salmela Architect
Photographer: Peter Kerze

Previous pages, the southwest façade of the tower provides views of Lake Superior. Above, the southeast façade with connecting bridge from the tower to the master bedroom. Following pages, the tower was positioned to take advantage of the views.

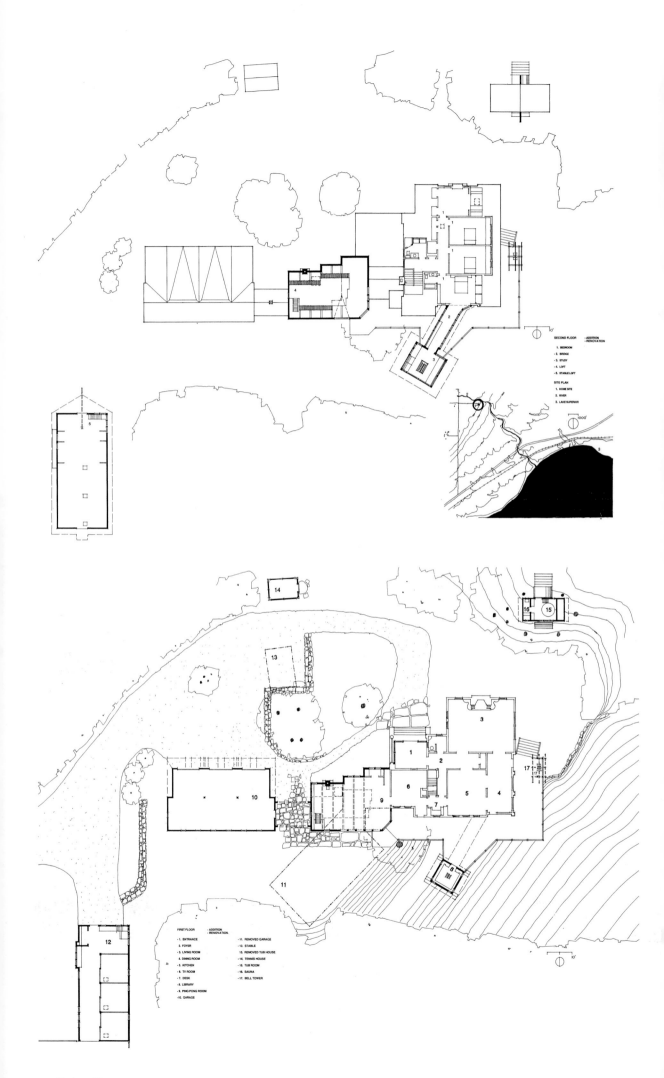

SECOND FLOOR · ADDITION
· RENOVATION

1. BEDROOM
2. BRIDGE
3. STUDY
4. LOFT
5. STABLE LOFT

SITE PLAN

1. HOME SITE
2. RIVER
3. LAKE SUPERIOR

FIRST FLOOR · ADDITION
· RENOVATION

1. ENTRANCE   11. REMOVED GARAGE
2. FOYER   12. STABLE
3. LIVING ROOM   13. REMOVED TUB HOUSE
4. DINING ROOM   14. TENNIS HOUSE
5. KITCHEN   15. TUB ROOM
6. TV ROOM   16. SAUNA
7. DESK   17. BELL TOWER
8. LIBRARY
9. PING PONG ROOM
10. GARAGE

30 Loken Tower

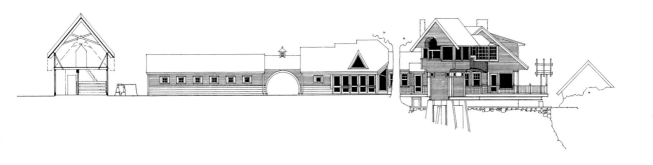

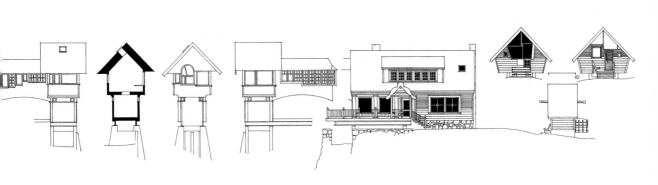

Left top, the bridge connecting the tower and the master bedroom. Left, underneath, the bridge provides shade in the summer. Above, view from the master bedroom to the office in the tower. Following pages, a ladder connects the tower's first floor library to the office.

Above, panoramic views await visitors to the tower's office.

Above and left, positioned on a steep slope, the tower becomes the dominant architectural feature of the house.

The architect built this tower as his primary residence on a difficult-to-build triangular lot in Chicago. The 1200-square-foot structure consists of an exposed steel tower on a 13-foot plan module and a 10-foot-square, 40-foot-tall concrete block stair tower that connects the four levels of the steel structure that contains the living quarters.

The fourth-floor roof terrace is the principal outdoor entertaining space and it provides a panoramic view of the dramatic Chicago skyline. Retractable, translucent awnings stretching across the top provide sun protection. Beneath the roof terrace are the loft-like living, dining, and kitchen spaces. A bedroom and guest room are located on the second level and the ground level has parking and covered access to the front door at the base of the concrete block tower. Large floor-to-ceiling steel-framed windows allow for unobstructed views and flood the rooms with light. Exterior walls are sheathed in horizontally-laid corrugated steel. New England slate floors are laid on light-weight concrete slabs containing hydronic heating elements.

The design of the steel frame of the tower is governed by Chicago building codes which prohibit unprotected steel structures. Consequently, 4-by-4 inch structure tubes are wrapped in 1-inch of fireproofing under an outer steel shell resulting in 6-by-6 inch columns. Because of this relatively slender structural support, the concrete tower is doubly reinforced and provides most of the racking support for the entire structure, allowing the steel tower to appear light and delicate. A bright red exterior circular staircase provides a second means of egress as required by code and further enhances the vertical pull of the steel tower.

Frederick Phillips & Associates
Photographer: Kildow Photography

Previous page, the structure consists of three components: the steel tower, the concrete block stair tower, and the exterior spiral staircase. Right, the east façade.

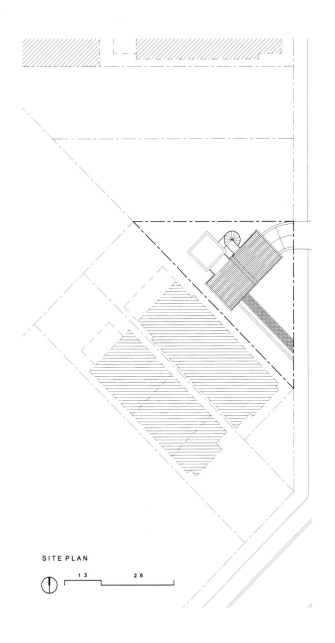

SITE PLAN

⊕ 1 3   2 6

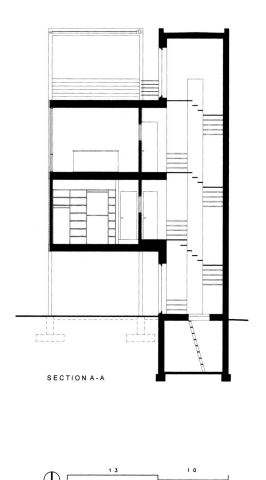

SECTION A-A

⊕ 1 3   1 0

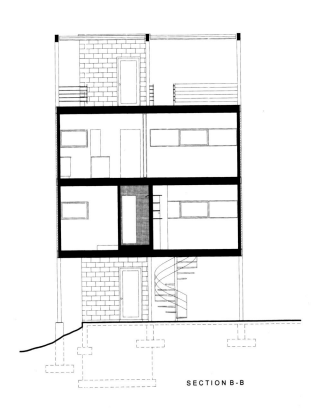

SECTION B-B

44 Tower House

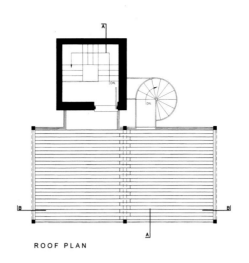

ROOF PLAN

THIRD FLOOR PLAN

SECOND FLOOR PLAN

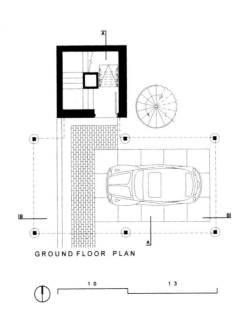

GROUND FLOOR PLAN

10   13

Previous pages and above, steel-framed glass window-walls provide unobstructed views of the Chicago skyline. Right, the concrete block tower contains the interior stairway and provides additional structural support for the minimalist steel living tower.

THE CISTERN

Sited on a hill in a prime residential neighborhood near Yale University this 365,000-gallon, century-old cistern stood abandoned until the current owners, an architect and a graphic designer, saw the opportunity to transform it into a Tuscan villa. In its raw state however, it was more like a fortress measuring 54 feet in diameter and 35 feet tall with 18-inch concrete walls, and of course, no windows. An attached octagonal stair tower winds up to what is now the roof deck.

Restoration began with attaching insulation to the exterior wall then applying a yellow-orange tinted stucco finish. Inside, the concrete walls were painted with a lime wash which hardened and stabilized the surface. Four existing concrete structural columns and the ceiling were sandblasted and left bare. The existing columns formed a 16-foot square in the center of the tower and provided the basis for the establishment of the room configurations. The owners are avid collectors of books so the entire interior space within the central core formed by the columns is organized around a two-story library. Rooms radiate from this square on the first floor and the newly created partial second floor.

Strategically located windows were saw-cut into the concrete wall and circular skylights were added to maximize the light that now reaches deep into the interior. Because of the thickness of the walls, bay windows were added in the kitchen and bedrooms in order to push the interior into the landscape.

Outside, this landscape retains a natural look, with with the addition of perennials and prairie grasses. A vine and canvas covered trellis rings the exterior wall of the south-facing living room. The canvas is suspended over the three large French door bays while the vines fall between the bays.

Peter de Bretteville, Architect
Photographer: Robert Benson

Previous pages, the octagonal stair tower; the trellised patio outside the living room. Above, steps leading to the entrance. Right, the trellis as seen from outside the kitchen.

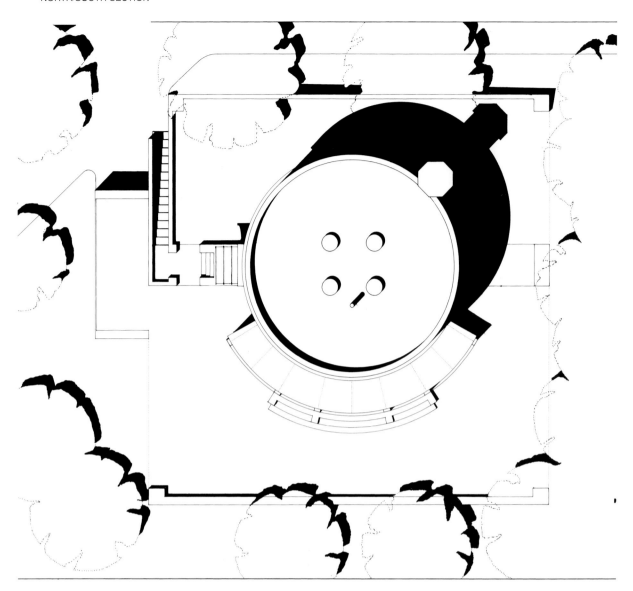

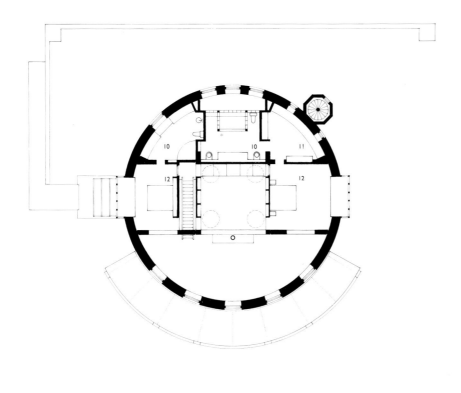

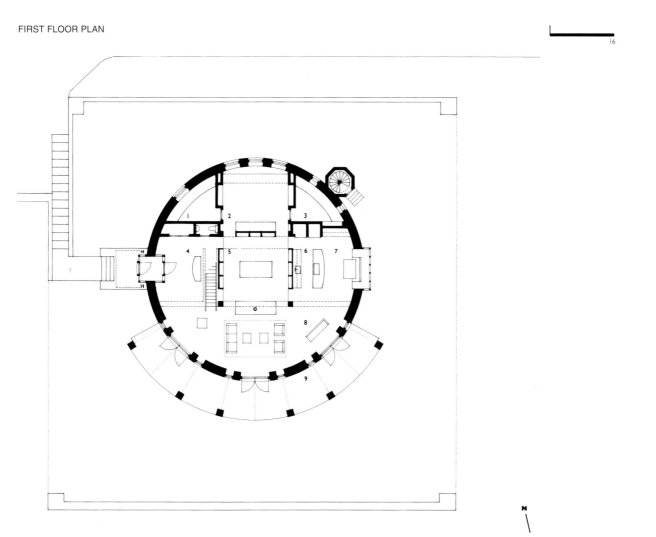

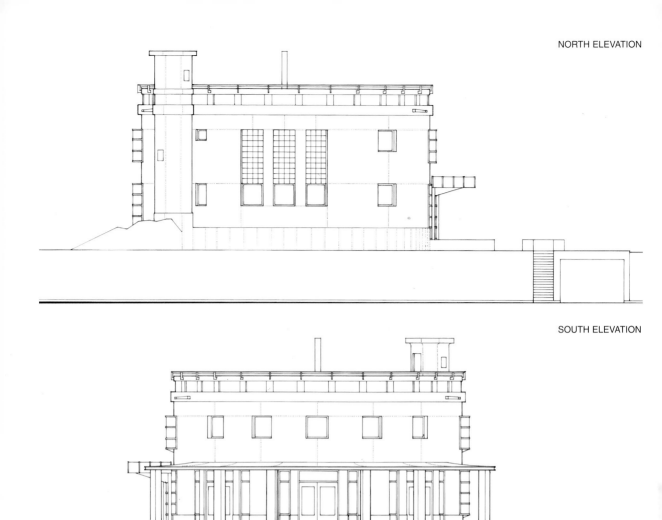

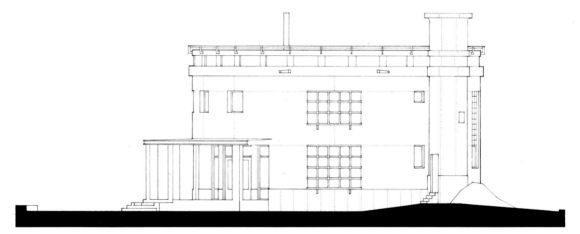

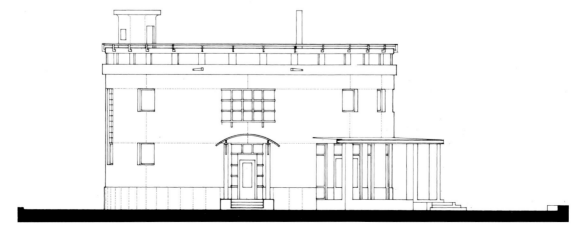

58 The Cistern

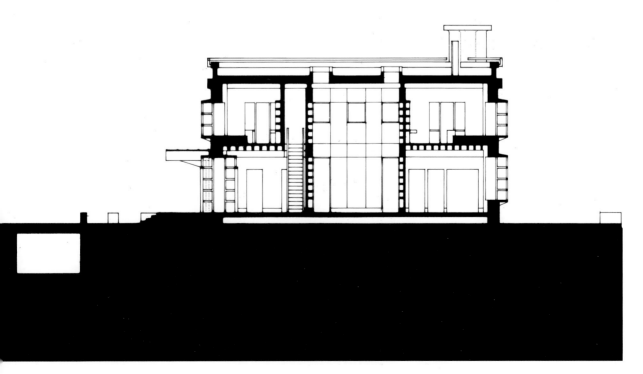

Previous pages, the living room; the two-story library; and the kitchen. Left and above, the library with a view of the steel and glass catwalk that connects the two bedrooms. Following pages, from it's perch on the hill, The Cisterr has unobstructed views.

VALLEY VIEW SILO

The 40-foot View Silo was designed to occupy the smallest practical footprint of earth and the narrowest possible sliver of sky. It is built on a 14-acre site at the edge of the cobbled alluvial fan of the Absoroka Mountains in Montana. The land is treeless, and the perfectly parabolic bank that dissects the property in a north-south line visually anchors the structure.

The region's grain silos and elevators provided inspiration for the design. As would be expected, the approximately 1500-square-foot program is organized vertically. Entry is at grade, with sleeping spaces below the crest of the bank, partially embedded in the earth. Immediately above are located the work and primary living spaces and as the silo narrows, a mezzanine for cooking and eating is located within the tapering double-height volume. On top of this space, the stair tower becomes open to the sky and is terminated at the rooftop observatory, its slatted perimeter providing a filtered 360-degree view while forcing the eye upward to the sky.

The building is clad on the south and east walls by a layered system of 2-by-2-inch pine slats reclaimed from pickling barrels. These vertical slats, which range in color from a slivery gray to a purplish black are layered over brick-red asphalt roll roofing for waterproofing. Future plans call for the installation of exterior shutters to protect the windows from severe storms and to present the quiet, uniform silhouette of the local grain silos. When opened, these shutters (illustrated on page 77) will also provide sun shading.

RoTo Architects
Photographer: Larry Stanley

Previous page, and above, the 1500-square-foot View Silo was designed to occupy the smallest practrical foot-print and the narrowest sliver of sky. Right, a view of the entrance to the ground floor guest quarters.

Left, view of living room windows and porch. Top, entrance. Above, porch detail.

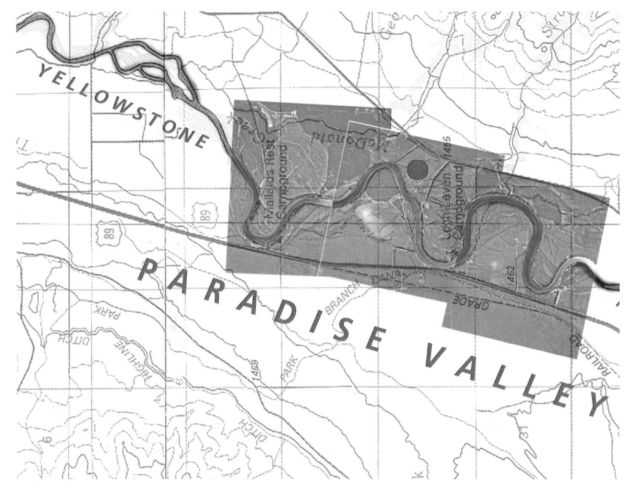

ROOF PLAN

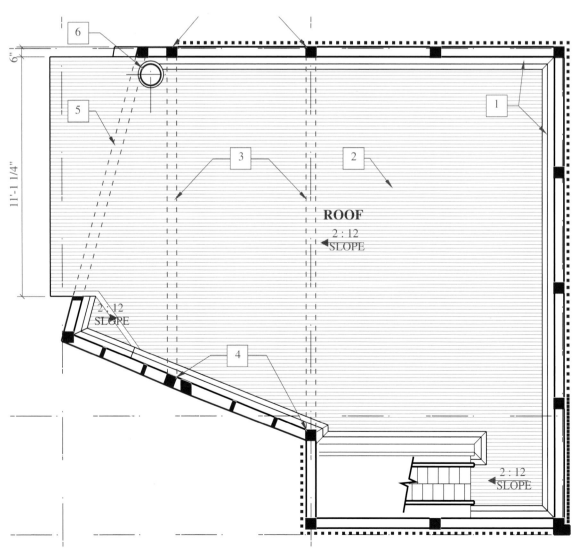

ROOF DECK

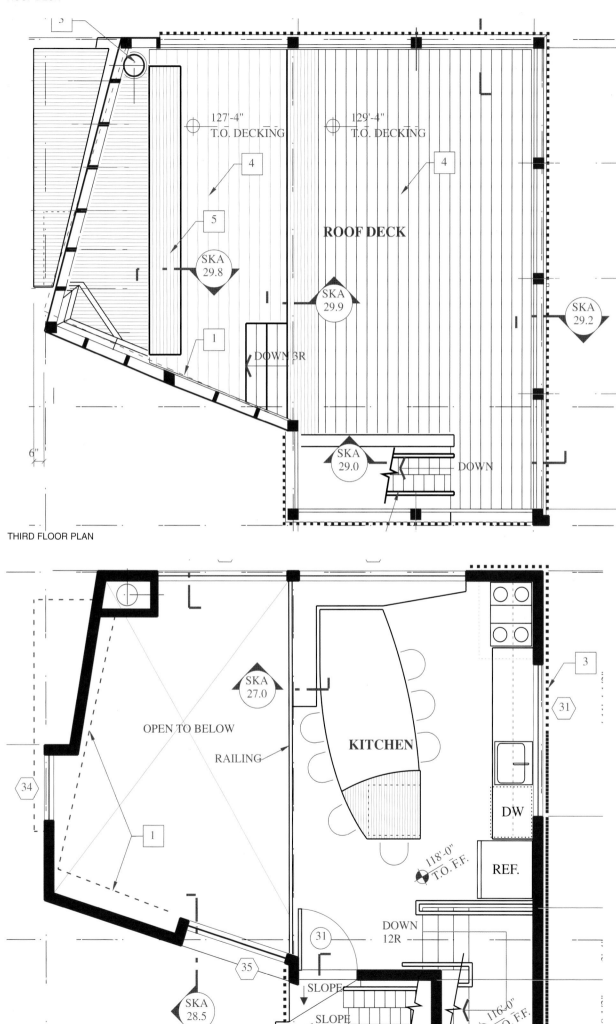

127'-4"
T.O. DECKING

129'-4"
T.O. DECKING

4

4

5

ROOF DECK

SKA
29.8

SKA
29.9

SKA
29.2

1

DOWN 3R

6"

SKA
29.0

DOWN

THIRD FLOOR PLAN

SKA
27.0

3

31

OPEN TO BELOW

KITCHEN

RAILING

34

DW

1

118'-0"
T.O. F.F.

REF.

31

DOWN
12R

35

SLOPE

SKA
28.5

SLOPE

4

116'-0"
T.O. F.F.

75

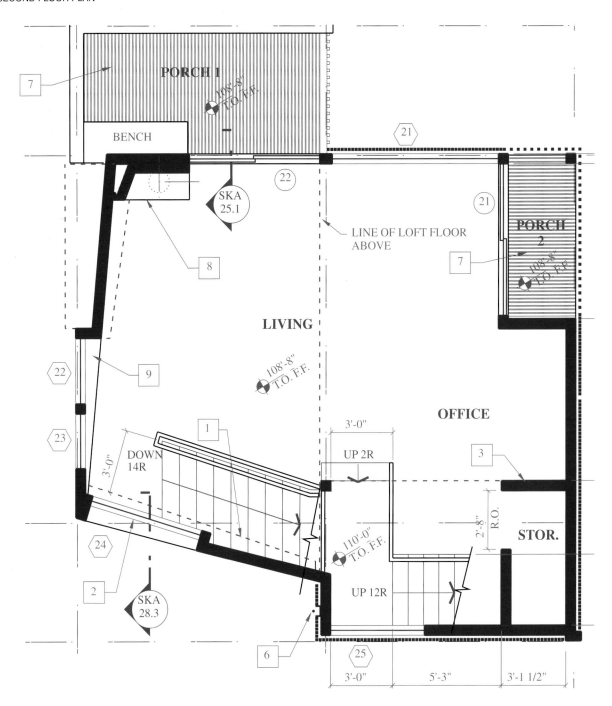

PORCH 1

108'-8"
T.O. F.F.

BENCH

7

21

22

SKA
25.1

LINE OF LOFT FLOOR
ABOVE

PORCH
2

21

7

108'-8"
T.O. F.F.

8

LIVING

108'-8"
T.O. F.F.

OFFICE

22

9

23

DOWN
14R

1

3'-0"

UP 2R

3

2'-8" R.O.

STOR.

3'-0"

24

2

110'-0"
T.O. F.F.

UP 12R

SKA
28.3

6

25

3'-0"

5'-3"

3'-1 1/2"

EAST ELEVATION (SHUTTERS CLOSED)   EAST ELEVATION (SHUTTERS OPEN)

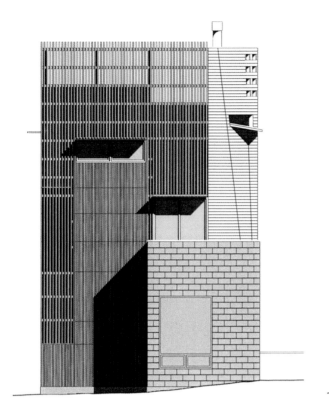 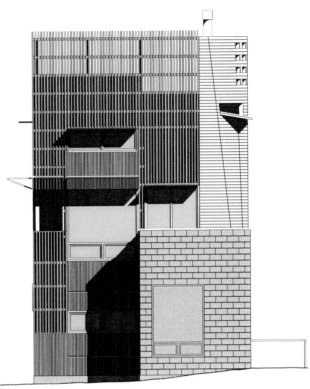

WEST ELEVATION   NORTH ELEVATION

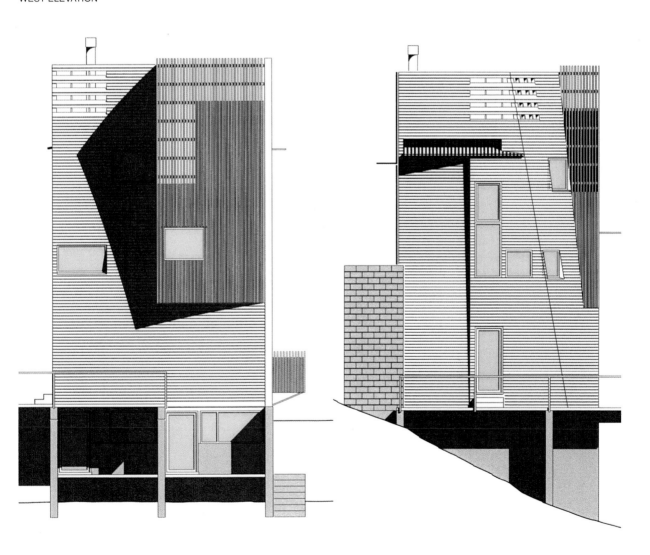

Previous pages, the master bedroom. Above, guest quarters/office are located on the ground floor accessible to the upstairs via a ships ladder.

Above and following pages, the living room with a view of the balcony where the kitchen (right) is located.

BELL TOWER

Rising 85 feet above an adjoining courtyard, the bell tower at the Mission Hill Family Estate is rich with iconographic references to the winemaker's family and the winery. The tower is constructed from precast concrete panels, integrally tinted to approximate the color of the 8500 cubic yards of rock that was removed to create the underground wine cellars beneath the tower and courtyard. Conceptually, the tower connects the cool, dark aging cellars to the richness of the earth and sky, referencing the natural qualities needed to create exceptional wine. Using one basic shape, the panels were fabricated and then assembled in a spiral puzzle fashion—rotated, flipped, or mirrored, and slightly clipped for the windows—to create the self-supporting tower. The strength of the tower is derived from this interlocking pattern eliminating the need for any framing.

A spiral staircase, located off a balcony just above the courtyard, provides access to the top of the tower. Each of the 87 tower steps is made using the same integrally colored concrete as the tower, with each step $^3/_{16}$ of an inch less in width than the step below it. This gradual tapering accentuates the sense of the tower's height as one ascends.

A viewing platform is positioned just below four bronze bells, handcrafted in Annecy, France by the Paccard Bell Foundry. Each bell is dedicated to a member of the proprietor's immediate family. A weather vane in the shape of a pelican, taken from the family crest, rests at the tower's peak.

Olson Sundberg Kundig Allen
Photographer: Paul Warchol

Previous page and above, constructed of interlocking precast concrete panels, the tower is selfsupporting.

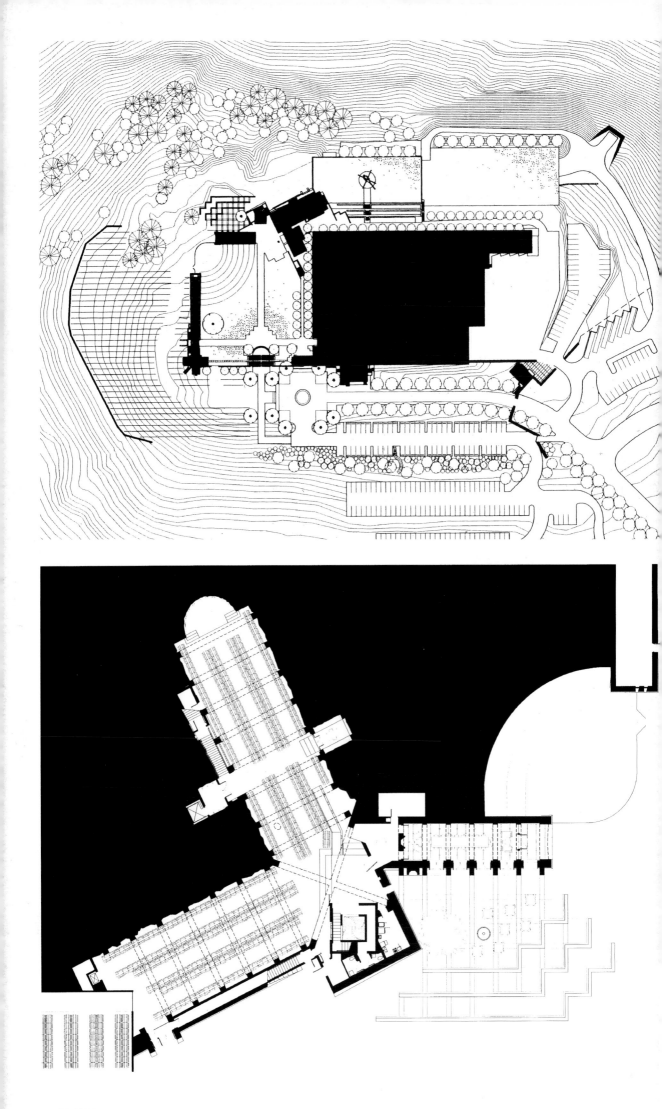

92 Bell Tower

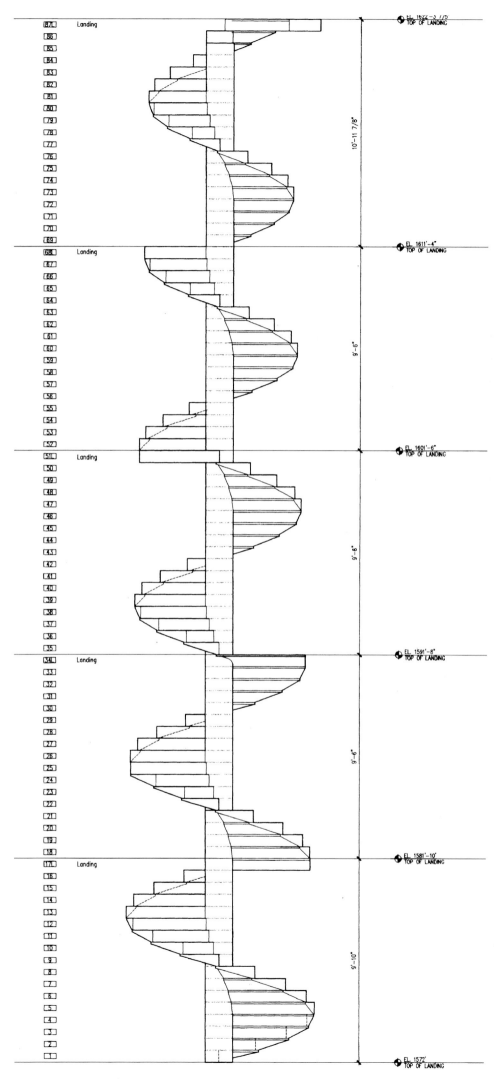

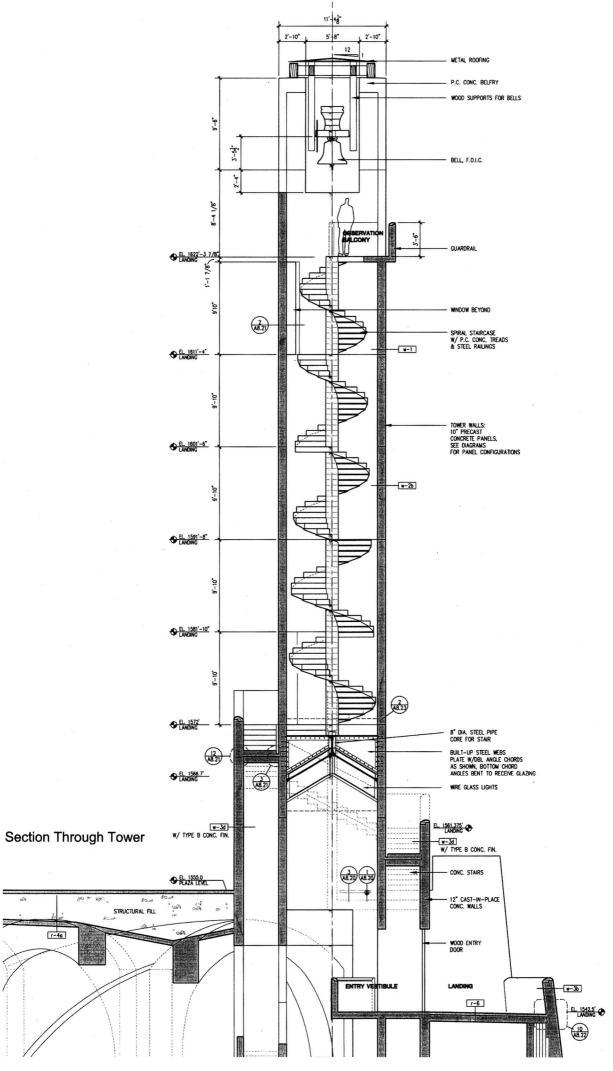

Section Through Tower

Labels (top to bottom, right side):

METAL ROOFING

P.C. CONC. BELFRY

WOOD SUPPORTS FOR BELLS

BELL, F.O.I.C.

GUARDRAIL

WINDOW BEYOND

SPIRAL STAIRCASE
W/ P.C. CONC. TREADS
& STEEL RAILINGS

TOWER WALLS:
10" PRECAST
CONCRETE PANELS,
SEE DIAGRAMS
FOR PANEL CONFIGURATIONS

8" DIA. STEEL PIPE
CORE FOR STAIR

BUILT-UP STEEL WEBS
PLATE W/DBL ANGLE CHORDS
AS SHOWN, BOTTOM CHORD
ANGLES BENT TO RECEIVE GLAZING

WIRE GLASS LIGHTS

CONC. STAIRS

12" CAST-IN-PLACE
CONC. WALLS

WOOD ENTRY
DOOR

Labels (left/interior):

OBSERVATION BALCONY

W/ TYPE B CONC. FIN.

STRUCTURAL FILL

ENTRY VESTIBULE

LANDING

W/ TYPE B CONC. FIN.

Elevations:

EL. 1622'-3 7/8" LANDING

EL. 1611'-4" LANDING

EL. 1601'-6" LANDING

EL. 1591'-8" LANDING

EL. 1581'-10" LANDING

EL. 1572' LANDING

EL. 1566.7' LANDING

EL. 1561.375' LANDING

EL. 1555.0 PLAZA LEVEL

EL. 1542.5' LANDING

Dimensions:

11'-4 1/8"

2'-10"   5'-8"   2'-10"

9'-6"

3'-5 1/2"

2'-4"

8'-4 1/8"

3'-6"

1'-1 7/8"

9'-10"

9'-10"

9'-10"

9'-10"

Detail markers: 2/A8.21, 2/A8.23, 12/A8.21, 3/A8.21, 3/A8.20, 1/A8.20, 10/A8.22

Wall tags: w-1, w-2b, w-3d, w-3b, r-4a, r-6

Above, 23 feet of the tower is concealed below ground. Right, a detail of the spiral staircase.

Above and right, an oculus placed in the central courtyard provides a glimpse of the cellars bellow. Once inside the cellars, the oculus serves as an orientation point.

Right, a view looking up the bell tower with the spiral staircase and its cross-like sturctural support visible. Above, the bells were handcrafted in France.

Left, a view into the wine cellars with the bell tower rising above them. Above, the viewing platform is located just below the bells. Following pages, the entry arch frames the tower.

Miners once claimed gold along the upper Arkansas River in Colorado where this architect's own retreat is located. It consists of four simple, elegant structures: a main cabin, guest cabin, a 50-foot-tall tower, and a recently added studio. The overall design achieves a remarkable connection with the natural environment. Ron Mason, a founding partner of AMD, purchased the land in 1973 and built the first structures a decade later after living for two summers on the land in a Sioux-style tipi.

Designed with the help of students from the University of Cincinnati and fabricated at the University's shop and on site, the tower has become a landmark for kayakers on this remote part of the river. The tower's structural frame consists of welded steel and diagonal cable bracing. The exterior skin is 2-by-6-inch southern yellow pine spaced to allow air and light to pass through. A stairway winds around the open center shaft of the tower leading to a platform under the tower room where final access is provided by a ladder and hatch. Built-in seating and storage converts to sleeping accommodations.

AndersonMasonDale Architects
Photographer: Greg Hursley

*Previous pages, the tower and adjacent structures were sited to take advantage of the natural landscape.
Above, the tower offers panoramic views of the river and rolling hills. Right, a view of the tower adjacent to
the newly constructed studio.*

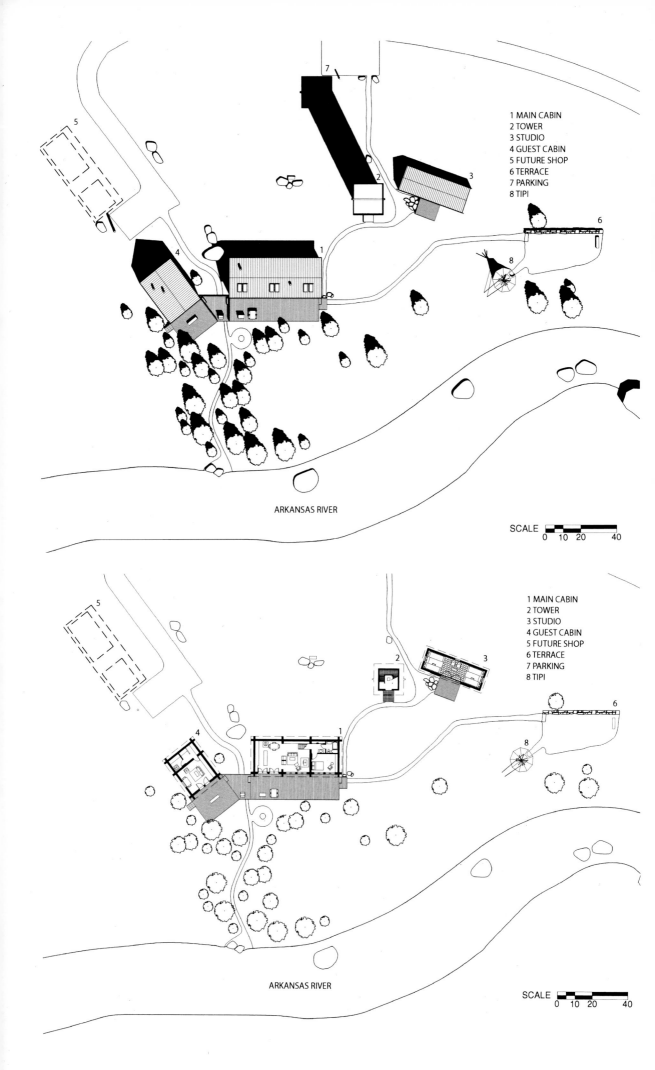

1 MAIN CABIN
2 TOWER
3 STUDIO
4 GUEST CABIN
5 FUTURE SHOP
6 TERRACE
7 PARKING
8 TIPI

ARKANSAS RIVER

SCALE
0 10 20 40

1 MAIN CABIN
2 TOWER
3 STUDIO
4 GUEST CABIN
5 FUTURE SHOP
6 TERRACE
7 PARKING
8 TIPI

ARKANSAS RIVER

SCALE
0 10 20 40

Right, a view of the studio from the tower's viewing platform.

Previous pages, looking up through the center of the tower, a glass panel is placed in the tower room offering the same view from above. Left and above, a steel stairway extends to a platform eight feet below the tower room where the final ascent is completed by ladder.

Above, the interior of the tower as seen from the viewing platform.
Right, the viewing platform as seen from the interior of the tower.
Following pages, the interior of the studio.

Above, both the main and guest cabins are constructed of 10-inch lodge-pole pine logs, which were cut from a standing dead forest on the Montana-Canada border and joined in the Swedish cope system. Left, the main cabin's living space is open and airy, with direct access to the deck overlooking the river. Following pages, a view of the entire compound and its relationship to the river.

YARDBIRD

The YardBird is a 240-square-foot elevated home office that provides a quiet retreat and isolated work environment. It is adjacent to the existing main residence and located less than a mile from Thomas Jefferson's Lawn at the University of Virginia in Charlottesville where the architect and future client met during their undergraduate years.

Inspired by the semi-industrial character of the neighborhood, the architect decided to forego the Jeffersonian neo-Classicism prevalent throughout much of this college town. Instead he took his inspiration from another architectural master, Le Corbusier. The continuous strip of steel-framed windows, the use of pilotis as structural elements, and straightforward corrugated metal siding pay homage to Le Corbusier and many of the nearby commercial buildings.

All horizontal interior surfaces including floors, desktops, and shelving are rendered in solid wood and rubber tile to provide durable, low maintenance work surfaces. The steel stair, awning windows, light fixtures, and storage systems are all stock items that help lower cost and speed construction.

Using standard construction materials and methods, the architect designed the 12-by-20-foot YardBird so that it can be easily modified to meet site specific circumstances, with a wide variety of interior configurations possible from an open plan studio space to custom work stations.

"Ultimately," the architect says, "It was our intention to create a structure that could function as a small out building or tool shed in the Virginia tradition while providing the more classical, aesthetic appeal of a garden folly."

Neal R. Deputy Architect
Photographer: Jim Rounsevell

Top, view of model from the east. Above, view of model from the west. Right top, a view of the existing house from YardBird. Right, a detail of the steel windows.

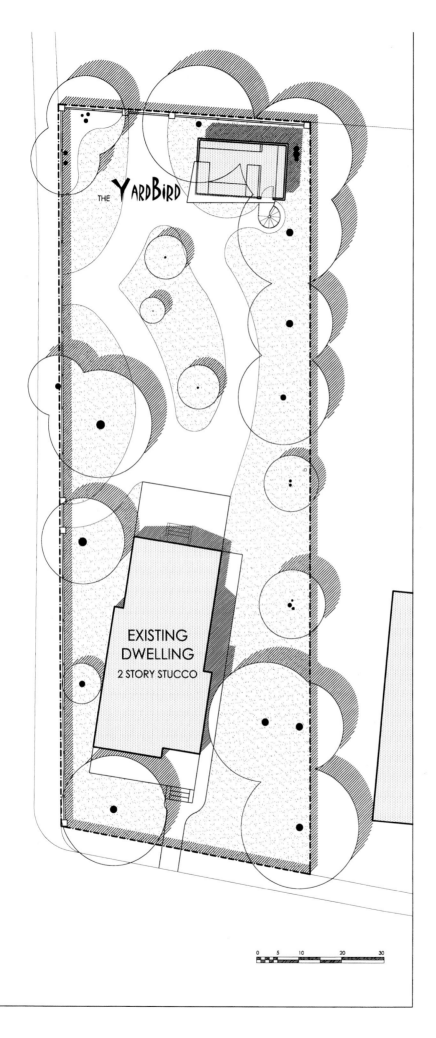

THE YARDBIRD

EXISTING
DWELLING
2 STORY STUCCO

0   5   10   20   30

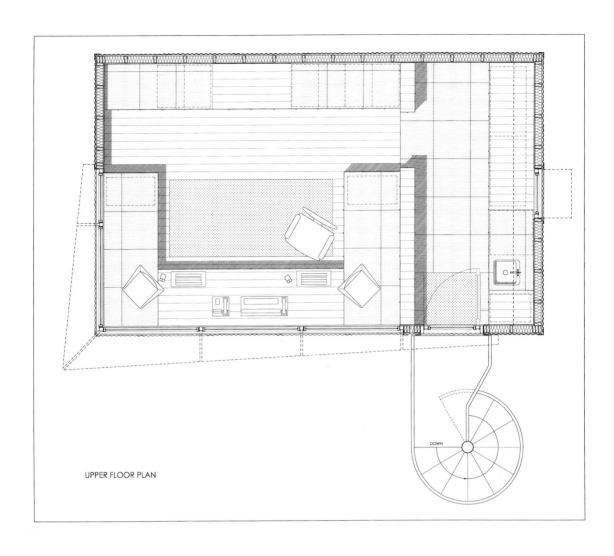

UPPER FLOOR PLAN

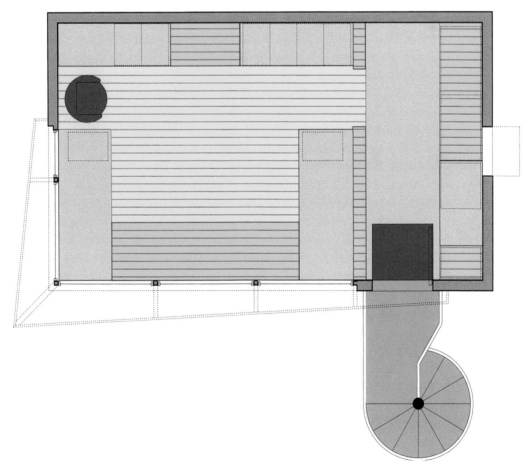

133

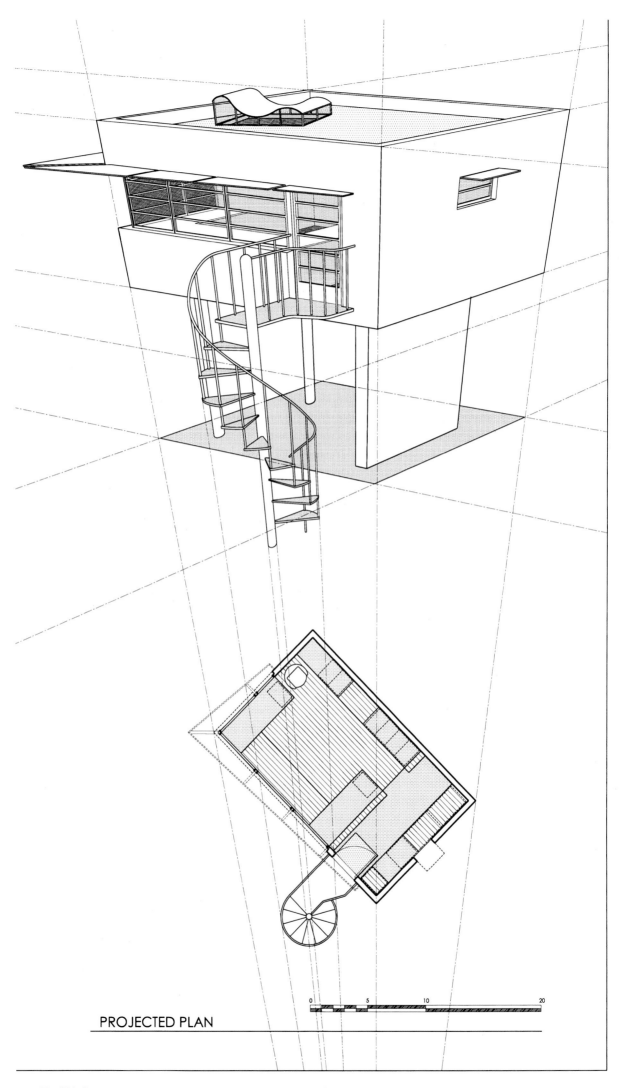

PROJECTED PLAN

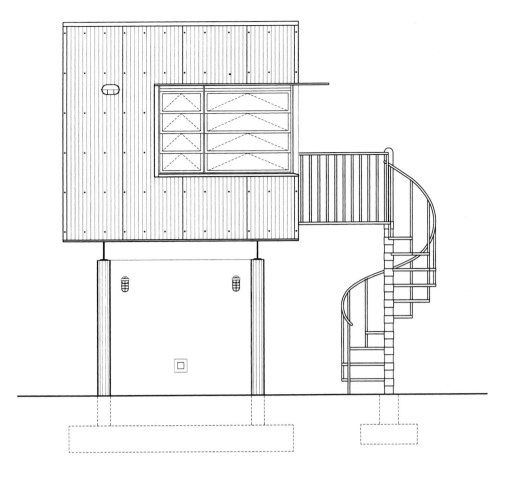

NORTH ELEVATION

1/2" = 1'-0"

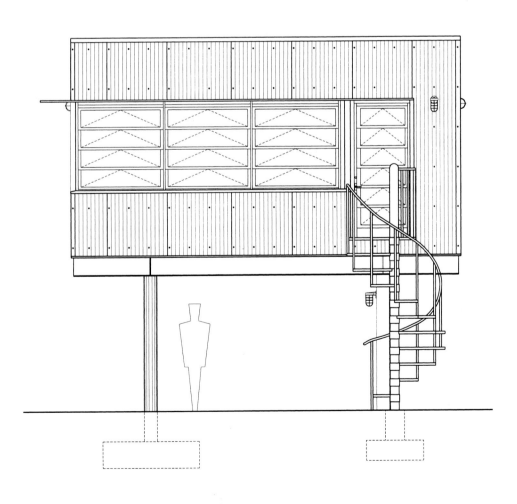

WEST ELEVATION

1/2" = 1'-0"

Right, view looking northwest.
Following pages, view of YardBird
from the main house.

Observatory House, a live/work space for an architect couple, was fashioned out of a craftsman-style bungalow in an old San Diego neighborhood. Built in the early 20th century, the house surrounds a courtyard filled with camellias, gardenias, and bougainvillea. In need of space for a large personal and professional book collection, the architects designed a tower in the form of a double height cube and positioned it at the front of the house.

Inside, the tower is lined from floor to ceiling with books. Small lateral windows are inserted between the bookshelves to admit shafts of light without compromising the privacy of the library. Shelves are set at various heights to accommodate books of different sizes as well as volumes of slides and a postcard collection. A dumbwaiter moves objects from the ground floor stacks up to the gallery-level reading room and on to the rooftop observatory. A steel stair with alternating treds facilitates carrying armloads of books to the reading room where there is a large built-in desk. A dutch door leads to a balcony with a cantilevered stair and on up to the rooftop observatory where there are views to San Diego's Balboa Park and the Pacific Ocean.

Davids Killory Architecture
Photographer: Undine Pröhl

Previous pages, the tower as viewed from the street; rectangular windows admit shafts of light into the tower. Above, glazing provides ample light for the reading room at the top. Right, view of the cantilevered stair to the rooftop observatory.

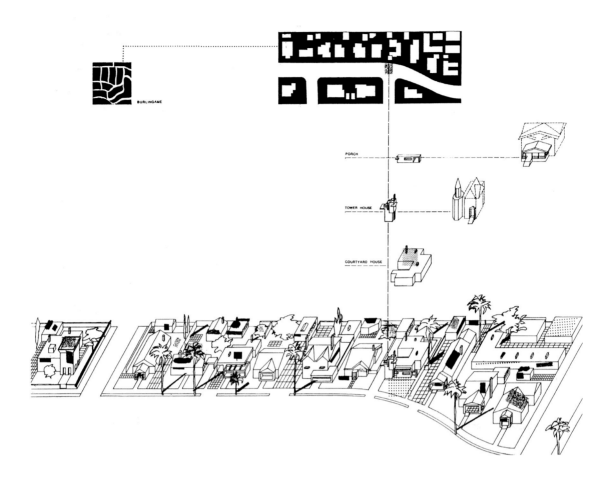

Right, access to the rooftop observator is via a ladder.

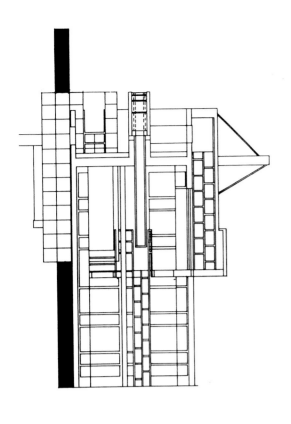
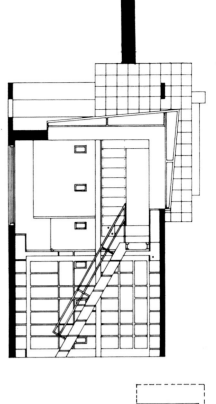

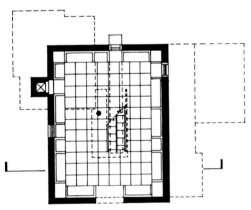
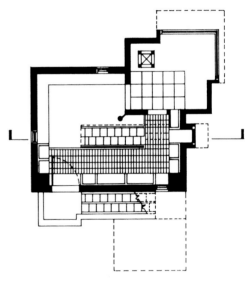

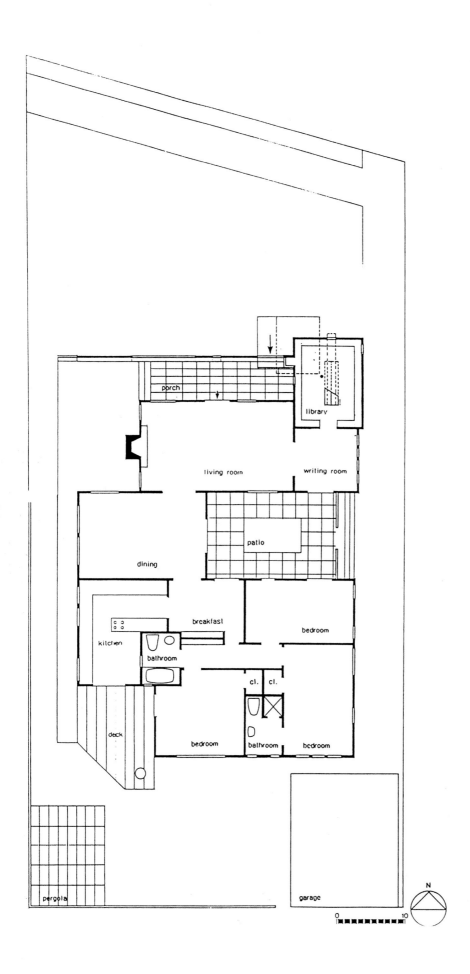

porch

library

living room

writing room

dining

patio

breakfast

bedroom

kitchen

bathroom

cl. cl.

deck

bedroom

bathroom

bedroom

pergola

garage

N

0 10

150 Observatory House

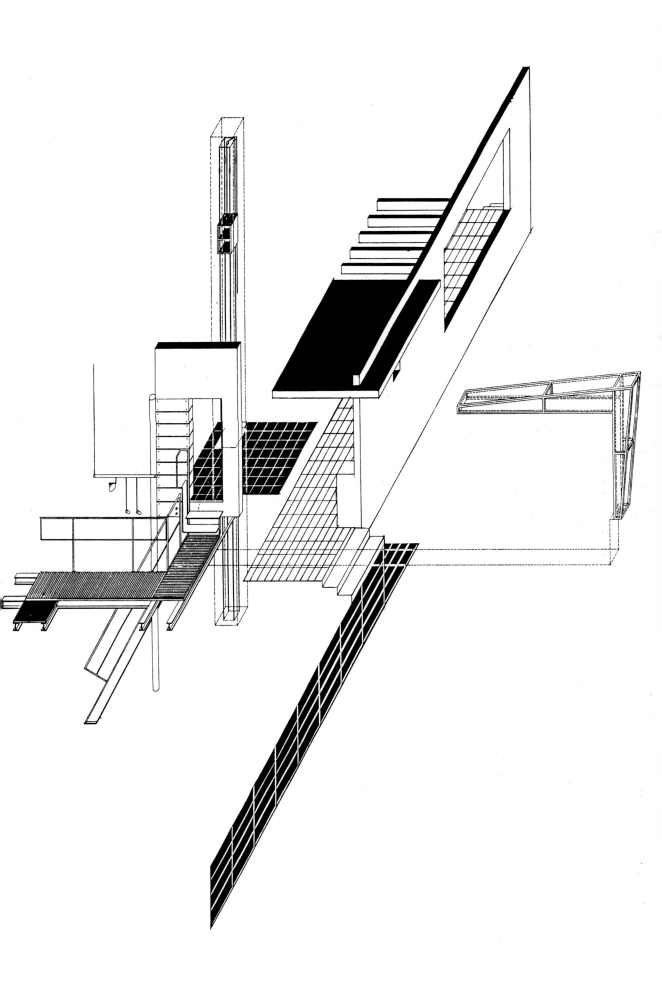

Left, the library with steel stairs to the reading room. Above, the reading room.

Above and right, the reading room with built-in desk.

FAYETTEVILLE TOWER

Recalling days spent in a tree house as a child, the architect's client wanted a vertical structure that would soar above the the the tree canopy and provide panoramic views of the surrounding Ozark mountain landscape. The resulting 82-foot Fayetteville Tower functions as a residential retreat, with four programmed levels: a utility room at 42 feet, a foyer, bathroom, and kitchenette at 50 feet, living/sleeping area at 57 feet, and finally, a skycourt for outdoor dining and observation at 69 feet.

Sited on a 57-acre wooded site, the steel tube tower structure is clad with a disengaged 2-by-6-inch vertical white oak fin lattice around the stairwell. The east elevation and upper program elements are clad in white standing-seam metal panels.

An open-air vertical sequence rotates up from the ground level covered with pecan shells, through the tree canopy to the foyer level where light and view are lost, and then regained upon entry into the light-filled living/sleeping room above. A fold down stair leads to the skycourt above. Here views are controlled through the specific placement of openings; the primary view is upward to the sky.

All wood floors, decks, and wall assemblies are of locally milled white oak. Mechanical, plumbing, and electrical lines are channeled through one vertical chase wall that also serves as structure for a small dumbwaiter. Only one tree was removed for the construction of the tower.

Marlon Blackwell Architect
Photographer: Timothy Hursley

Previous page, above, and right, clad in vertical white oak fin lattice and standing-seam steel panels, the tower relates to the surrounding natural and industrial environments.

Left, detail of the vertical lattice. Top and above, view of entrance into courtyard of creek stones and pecan shells.

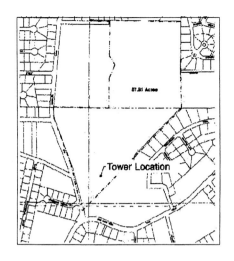

Tower Location

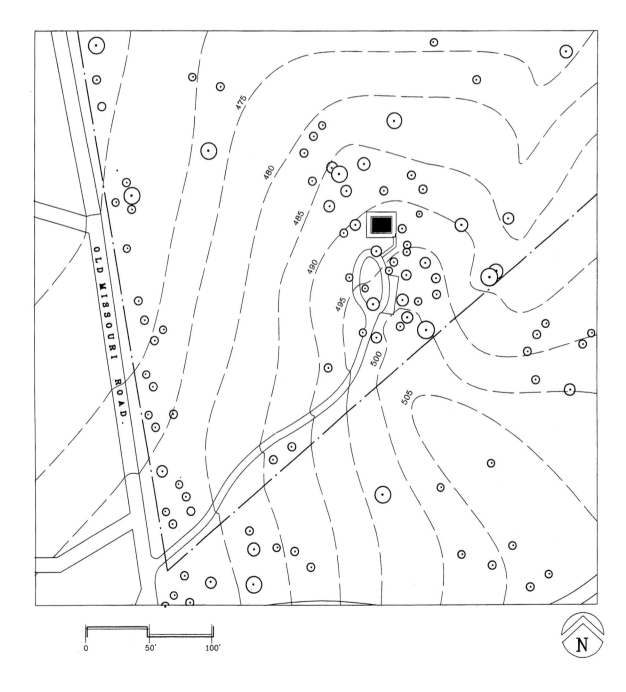

OLD MISSOURI ROAD

N

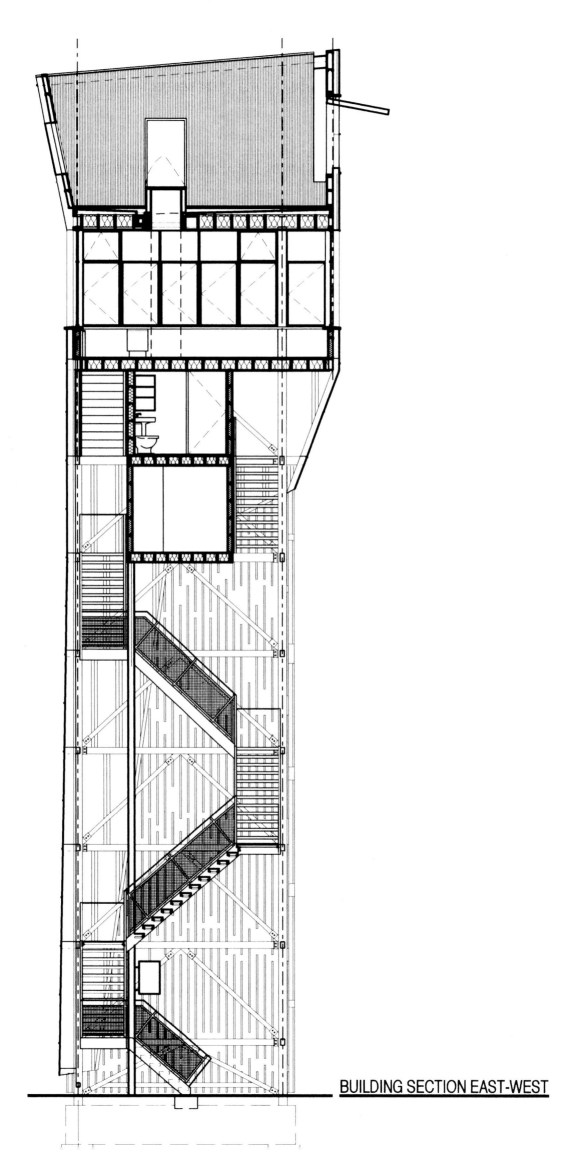

BUILDING SECTION EAST-WEST

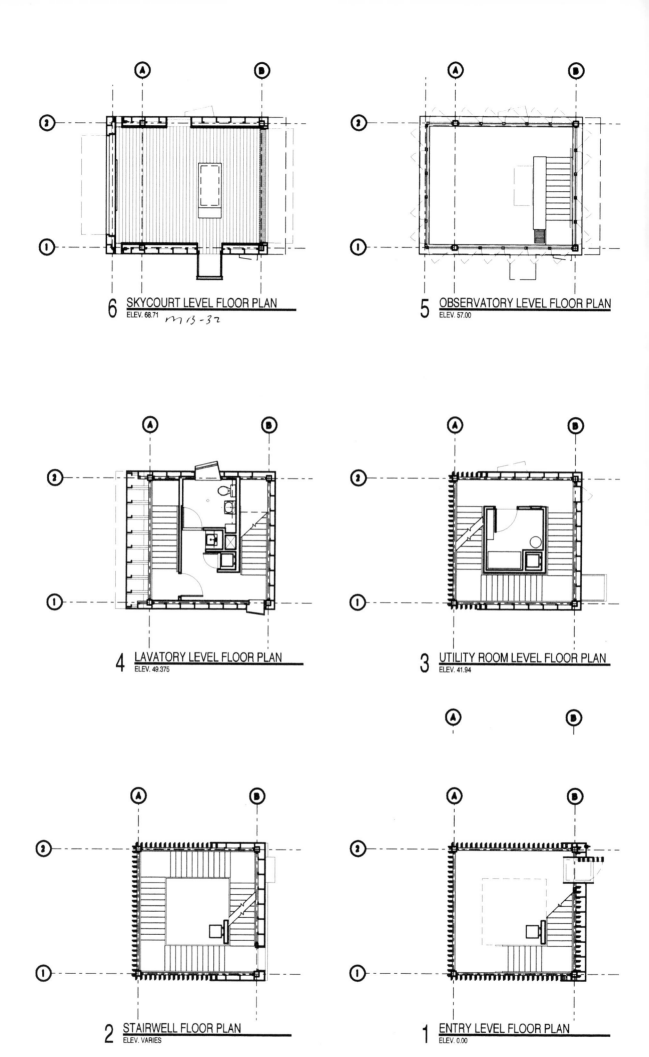

6 SKYCOURT LEVEL FLOOR PLAN
ELEV. 68.71 ᵐ₁₃-₃₂

5 OBSERVATORY LEVEL FLOOR PLAN
ELEV. 57.00

4 LAVATORY LEVEL FLOOR PLAN
ELEV. 49.375

3 UTILITY ROOM LEVEL FLOOR PLAN
ELEV. 41.94

2 STAIRWELL FLOOR PLAN
ELEV. VARIES

1 ENTRY LEVEL FLOOR PLAN
ELEV. 0.00

Left, interior view of the stairwell with vertical chase wall and dumbwaiter. Above, the open staircase.

Above, the interior staircase leading to the living/sleeping area.
Right, panoramic views dominate the minimally furnished
living/sleeping area.

Above, right and following pages, on the roof deck, views are carefully controlled through the specific placement of openings.

TIMBER TOWER

Inspired by the rudimentary constructions of the Pawnee Indians and by the vernacular forms such as grain silos that dot this flat, Kansas landscape, the architect designed the Terrace House to promote a harmonious balance between the powerful forces of nature in this region—wind, dust, tornadoes—and the built environment.

The site is a 30-acre terraced field of brome grass, barren of trees except for in an area along a creek at the west edge of the property. The house is built on a concrete plinth that extends parallel to the terraces at a continuous elevation.

In contrast to the subterranean feel of the entry, the main living area, which includes the kitchen and living room, surround a 32-foot high tower with a dramatic timber structure consisting of 10-by-10-inch Douglas fir columns. At the peak of the tower are operable skylights that provide ventilation and that funnel light into the house, creating a rich tapestry of shadows along the walls and floor.

Radiating from this vertical anchor are the wings of the house containing bedrooms, offices, and a guest room. These wings have deep overhangs that provide shade and emphasize the horizontality of the landscape. The swimming pool is visible form nearly every room in the house.

Rockhill and Associates
Photographer: Dan Rockhill

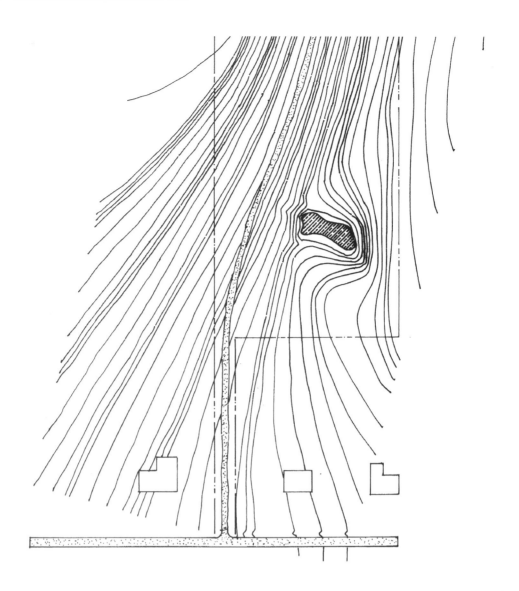

180 Timber Tower

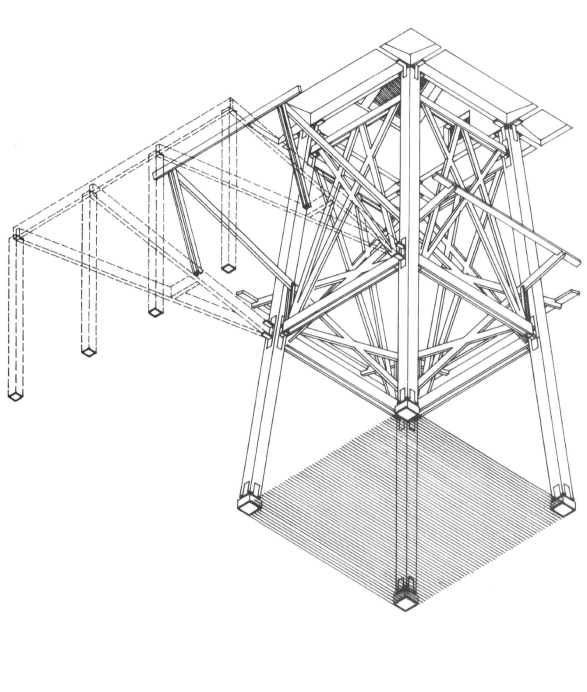

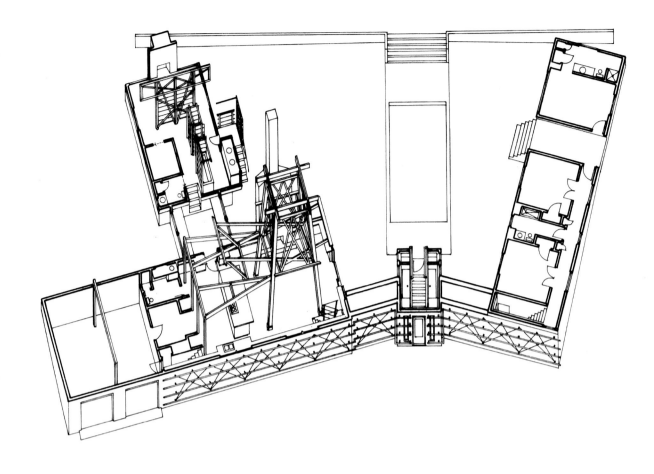

Left, the tower under construction.
Right, a view of the entrance.

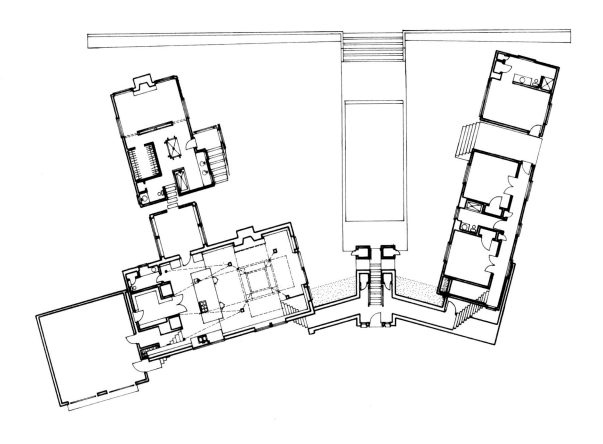

Above, the operable skylights at the top of the tower bring light into the room and provide ventilation. Right, the kitchen and living room are contained within the tower.

Above, the stair railings, shower and bath surrounds, and the visual screen for the master bedroom are sculptural elements made with oak and glass. Right, a large island with red travertine countertop resting on maple cabinets defines the kitchen area. Following pages, a view of the garages, tower, and main entrance.

RURAL STUDIO SILO

Abandoned silos dot the fields of this rural southern landscape, their useful lives long since past. However, one of these silos is enjoying a new life as an office and viewing platform thanks to the ingenuity of a student in the Rural Studio program at Auburn University. The Rural Studio, co-founded by the late Samuel Mockbee and it's current director D.K. Ruth, is internationally known for designing housing for poor residents of Hale County, Alabama.

This silo, one of the first projects of the Studio, is approximately 40 feet high and 20 feet in diameter and is located on a large catfish farm in Alabama. The student, Scott Rae, designed an all glass structure surrounded by a walkway to sit atop the silo. A steel cage with separate footings was constructed around the silo. The glass structure was assembled on the ground and then lifted by crane to the top of the silo and attached to the steel cage. Access is via a doorway at the base of the silo that leads to an interior stair to the office and viewing platform.

Rural Studio, Auburn University
Scott Rae, student
Photographer: D.K. Ruth

Pencil House
Akira Yoneda, Architect
Masahiro Ikeda(MIAS),
Structural Designer
1-7-16-612 Honcho
Shibuya, Tokyo, Japan 151-0071
Tel: 81-3-3374-0846
Fax: 81-3-5365-2216
a-tecton@pj8.s0-net.ne.jp

Loken Tower
David Salmela, Architect
852 Grandview Avenue
Duluth, MN 55812
Tel: (218) 724-7513
Fax: (218) 728-6805

Tower House
Frederick Phillips & Associates
1456 North Dayton
Chicago, IL 60622
Tel: (312) 255-0415
Fax: (312) 255-0446

The Cistern
Peter de Bretteville, Architect
315 Peck Street
Building 24, Unit 2G
New Haven, CT 06513
Tel: (203) 785-0586
Fax: (203) 785-0612
pdeb@pdebarc.com

Valley View Silo
RoTo Architects, Inc.
600 Moulton Avenue
Los Angeles, CA 90031
Tel: (323) 226-1112
Fax: (323) 226-1105

Bell Tower
Olson Sundberg Kundig Allen
    Architects
108 First Avenue South
Fourth Floor
Seattle, Washington 98104
Tel: (206) 624-5670
Fax: (206) 624-3730
www.olsonsundberg.com

Georgia Bar
AndersonMasonDale Architects
1615 Seventeenth Street
Denver, Colorado 80202
Tel: (303) 294-9448
Fax: (303) 294-0762
amd@amdarchitects.com

YardBird
Neal R. Deputy Architect Inc.
520 Lincoln Road
Miami Beach, FL 33139
Tel: (305) 534-4020
Fax: (305) 534-4095
nrdai@aol.com

Observatory House
Davids Killory Architecture
5866 Pladeau Street
Emeryville, CA 94608
Tel: (510) 601-7862
Fax: (510) 601-7863
davikill@pacbell.net

Fayetteville Tower
Marlon Blackwell, Architect
100 W. Center, Suite 001
Fayetteville, AR 72701
Tel: (501) 973-9121

Timber House
Rockhill and Associates
1546 E. 350 Road
Lecompton, Kansas 66050
Tel: (785) 864-4024
Fax: (785) 887-3936
drockhil@ku.edu

Rural Studio Silo
Dennis K. Ruth, Director
Scott Rae, student
115 Dudley Commons
Auburn University, Alabama 36849
Tel: (334) 844-5426
Fax: (334) 844-5458